BACH FAMILY

A BACH FAMILY ALBUM

Edited by Richard Jones

THE ASSOCIATED BOARD OF
THE ROYAL SCHOOLS OF MUSIC

INTRODUCTION

This edition consists of twenty pieces – Minuets and Polonaises, together with a single Aria – selected from the manuscript Mus. ms. Bach P 672 (Staatsbibliothek Preussischer Kulturbesitz, West Berlin). P 672 was apparently copied from a collection of little keyboard pieces by members of the Bach family, including Bach's son-in-law, Johann Christoph Altnickol (1719-59). The title reads:

Kleine Clavier=Stücke. / von / J.S. Bach. / C.P.E. Bach. / J.C. Bach. / J.C.F. Bach. / Altnickol

The copy was made by Michel, a Hamburg copyist of C.P.E. Bach's, and probably dates from the 1780s. It may be identical with, or derived from, a manuscript described in the catalogue of C.P.E. Bach's estate (Hamburg, 1790) as:

Ein kleines Büchlein, worinn ausser von C.P.E. auch von Johann Sebastian und Johann Christian (dem Londner) Bach verschiedene Sing- und Clavier-Compositionen eingeschrieben sind.

(Cited from the facsimile edition, ed. R.W. Wade, New York & London, 1981.) Among the contents are some of the earliest compositions – six Minuets, two Polonaises and an Aria – by Johann Christian (1735-82), the youngest son of Johann Sebastian Bach. In addition, the manuscript contains the Polonaise from J.S. Bach's orchestral Suite No. 2 in B minor, BWV 1067, in a keyboard version in D minor, which also exists in the form of an album entry in Johann Christian's hand, dated 23rd October, 1748 (see H.-J. Schulze: 'Frühe Schriftzeugnisse der beiden jüngsten Bach-Söhne', Bach-Jahrbuch, L (1963-4), pp.61 ff.).

The association of the manuscript P 672 with the album entry of 1748, the presence within it of some of J.C. Bach's earliest pieces, and the contributions of Altnickol, all point to an origin in a collection of pieces compiled within the Bach household between about 1744 and 1748 – the period in which Altnickol was a pupil of Bach's in Leipzig. Johann Christian Bach's age at that time – between about nine and thirteen – accords with the obvious educational purpose of the collection. Indeed, Schulze (in the above-mentioned article) raises the possibility that the original took the form of a 'Clavierbüchlein vor Johann Christian Bach'.

A complete list of the contents of P 672 can be found in Paul Kast's catalogue *Die Bach-Handschriften der Berliner Staatsbibliothek* (Trossingen, 1958). The present selection includes:

1. Three of the seven pieces by Johann Sebastian Bach (1685-1750): the aforenamed Polonaise in D minor, and what may be early versions of the two Minuets from keyboard Partita No. 1 in B flat major, BWV 825; the other four – little Preludes, BWV 933-4 & 937-8 – have been omitted on the grounds that they are already present in a recently published Associated Board edition (J.S. Bach: *A Little Keyboard Book*, ed. Richard Jones, London, 1988).

2. Both of the pieces by (or attributed to) Carl Philipp Emanuel Bach (1714-88) – a Minuet in E flat and a Polonaise in G – neither of which is listed in A. Wotquenne's *Thematisches Verzeichnis der Werke von Carl Philipp Emanuel Bach (1714-1788)*, Leipzig, 1905 (a new thematic catalogue by E. Helm is in preparation).

3. All five pieces by Johann Christoph Friedrich, the 'Bückeburg Bach' (1732-95) – Minuets in F, G and A, and Polonaises in F and G (Nos. XII/8-12 in H. Wohlfarth's catalogue in his *Johann Christoph Friedrich Bach*, Berne, 1971).

4. Seven of the nine pieces by Johann Christian Bach (all but the weakest: the Minuets with trio in C and G minor; none of these pieces is listed in C.S. Terry's catalogue in his *John Christian Bach* (London, 1929), but they are included in the work-list in *The New Grove* and have recently been published in a modern edition (J.C. Bach: *Kleine Klavierstücke*, ed. Susanne Staral, Graz, 1981).

5. One of the seven pieces by Altnickol: a Minuet in C (the others are two Minuets in B flat, Minuets in F and E flat, and Polonaises in C and D minor).

6. Two of the thirteen anonymous pieces: a Polonaise in G minor (Kast: Bach-Incerta 28) and a Minuet in G (Kast: Incerta 89).

In this practical edition, the soprano clef of the original is replaced by the treble clef throughout; original words are roman, editorial words in italics; and all secondary signs – phrasing, fingering, ornaments and dynamics – are editorial unless otherwise stated in footnotes. Where typographically distinguished, editorial signs are given in small print or within square brackets. The editor would like to express his gratitude to the Musikabteilung, Staatsbibliothek Preussischer Kulturbesitz, Berlin (West) for kindly providing microfilm of the original manuscript.

RICHARD JONES
Oxford, 1988

BACH FAMILY ALBUM

POLONOISE

di J. C. Bach

[♩ = c.69]

POLONOISE 2

J. S. Bach

[♩ = c.66]

A keyboard version of the Polonaise from the Orchestral Suite No.2 in B minor for flute, strings and continuo, BWV 1067. The large ornaments and staccatos are present in the source; the small ones, together with the tempo mark, dynamics and slurs, are borrowed from the orchestral version.

B.5, 1st bass note in the original: *b* flat, not *a*, in error.

Bb.9 & 10, ornament to 5th treble note in the original: mordent, not shake.

MENUETTO

J. C. Bach

[♩ = c.120]

MENUETTO

C. P. E. Bach

The slur to the triplet in b.9 is present in the source.

[♩ = c.112]

MENUETTO

J. C. Bach

The trill in b.2 is present in the source.

[♩ = c.100]

ARIA

J. C. Bach

Andante cantabile

[♩ = c.88]

MENUETTO

J. C. Bach

[♩ = c.120]

The slurs of b.12 are present in the source. B.8a (1st time bar) is editorial; b.16b (2nd time bar) is indicated in the MS by a pause to the bass crotchet
d in b.16a.

POLONOISE

J. C. Bach

B.14, last bass note: *c* not *B* flat in the original.

[♩ = *c.***100**]

MEN[UETTO]

di Altnickol

AB 2042

The large ornaments are present in the source, the small ones editorial.

[♩ = c. 120]

MENUETTO

J. C. Bach

Bb.1 & 13, l.h., beats 2 & 3: *c* & *d* in the original, but cf. b.9.

B.11, 2nd bass note in the original: *c* not *d*.

POLONOISE

Anon.

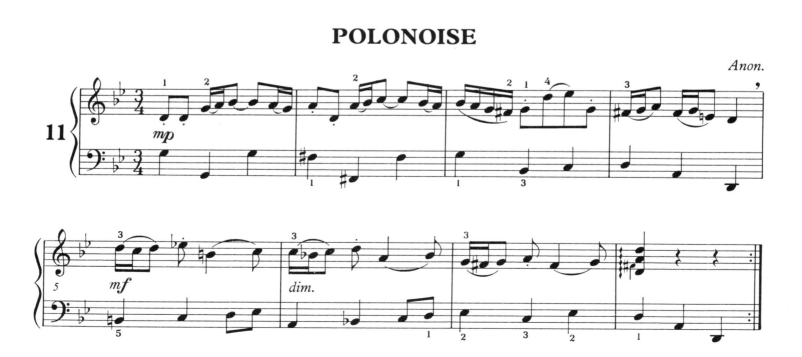

Rhythms in the original: b.2, r.h., beats 2–3: ♩♪♪♪♩♪♪ ; bb.4 & 12, r.h., beat 2: ♩♪♪ .

B.7, 3rd bass note: *d*, not *e* flat, in the original.

MENUETTO

J. S. Bach

Probably an early version of the 2nd Minuet from Partita No.1 in B flat, BWV 825. The staccatos and ornaments are borrowed from the Urbana (Illinois, U.S.A.) exemplar of the original edition of *Clavierübung* I (Leipzig, 1731).

B.6, 1st beat: plus crotchet *d′* in the original, tied over from the previous bar.

MEN[UETTO]

di J. S. Bach

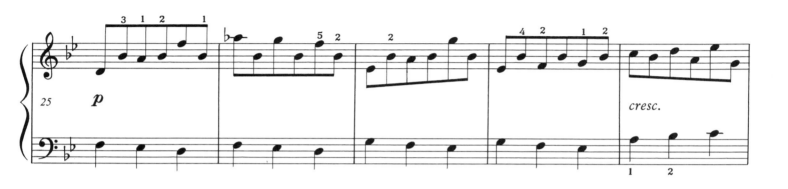

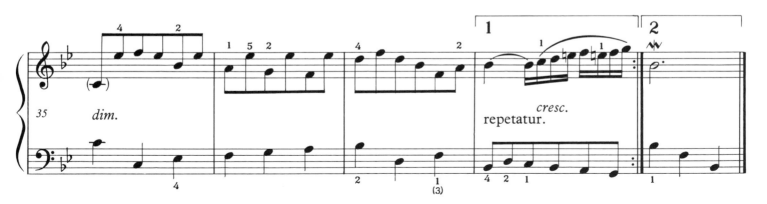

Probably an early version of the 1st Minuet from Partita No.1 in B flat, BWV 825.

The slurs and mordents are editorial.

POLONOISE

J. C. F. Bach

The large trills are present in the source, the small ones editorial.

MENUETTO

J. C. F. Bach

The only ornament in the original is the trill in b.13.

The dotted rhythms should be assimilated to the triplets by executing them thus:

The dots in the l.h. of b.16, which are present in the source, signify not staccato but equal quavers.

POLONOISE

J. C. F. Bach

[♩ = c.**88**]

3rd bass note of b.6 in the original: *d* not *c*, but cf. b.2.

MENUETTO

J. C. F. Bach

[♩ = c.**120**]

The only slur in the source is that of b.15.

3rd crotchet of b.10, l.h.: *d* not *a* in the original.

2nd crotchet of b.11, l.h.: crotchet rest in the original.

MENUETTO

J. C. F. Bach

The dotted rhythm 𝅘𝅥𝅮. 𝅘𝅥𝅯 should be softened to 𝅘𝅥 𝅘𝅥𝅮 throughout in order to assimilate it to the triplets.

The slurs in b.5 and the appoggiatura in b.16 are present in the source.

Bass, bb.14–15, 1st crotchet: 3rd higher in the original.

POLONOISE

di C. P. E. Bach

The grace notes and the slurs to the triplets are present in the source. The 2nd time bar (b.8b) is editorial.

[♩ = c.88]

MENUETTO

Anon.

[♩ = c.132]

Processed and printed by
Halstan & Co. Ltd., Amersham, Bucks., England